SECRET MAGNETS

by HERMAN and NINA SCHNEIDER

illustrated by
TĀLIVALDIS STUBIS

SCHOLASTIC INC.
New York Toronto London Auckland Sydney

To our grandchildren, in alphabetical order:
Adam, Benjie, Daisy, David, Debbie,
Jennifer, and Michaela.

ISBN 0-590-05769-3

12 11 10   0/9

Printed in the U.S.A.   08

Contents

Everywhere a Magnet

How many magnets are in your house?
None? One? More than one?
How about a hundred?

Even a small house has more than
a hundred magnets!
Most of them are hidden.
But you can track them down.

One magnet is in the back of this book.
This magnet is called a bar magnet.
Take your bar magnet and walk around the room.

Touch the magnet to different things in the room.
Some things will stick to the magnet.
These things are attracted to it.
Some things are not attracted to the magnet.

6

Did your magnet attract these things?
They look very different.
Yet they are alike in one way.
They all have iron or steel in them.
(Steel is a special hard kind of iron.)
Magnets attract iron and steel.

Magnet number one was in the back of this book.
How about those hundreds of other magnets
in your house?
Most of them are hidden.
They are covered with something else.
Can you find a magnet through a cover?
That depends on the cover.

Cover your magnet with this book.
Put a paper clip on top of the book.
(The paper clip is made of steel.)
Move the magnet back and forth, under the book.
The paper clip follows the magnet!

There is a force in the magnet.
The force is called magnetism.
You can't see magnetism,
but you can see what it does.
Magnetism passes through paper
and moves the paper clip.

Does magnetism pass through glass?
Put a paper clip inside the glass.
Then try to make the paper clip move around.

Does magnetism pass through plastic?
How about a penny?
Try other coins. You may be surprised.

Does magnetism pass through water?
Put some water in a glass.
Drop a paper clip in it and find out.

Here's another way to find out.
Cut an empty milk carton to make some fish.
Put a paper clip on each fish head.
Have a good fishing trip!

Isn't there something that stops magnetism?
Try a steel baking dish or pie pan.
Try an empty tin can.
(A tin can is made of steel covered with tin.)

Make a Magnet Detector

You've seen that magnetism passes through
paper, glass, plastic—even water.
Now you are ready to go snooping for magnets.
But first you have to make a magnet detector.

You will need:
your bar magnet,
five sewing needles,
five minutes.

To find a magnet you need a magnet.
So first make some needle magnets.
Lay three needles side by side —
eyes together and points together.
Stroke them with one end of the magnet.
Stroke them from eye to point.

Always move the same way, from eye to point.
Fifty times would be good.
If you get bored, thirty times will do.

The needles don't look any different.
But you have changed them.
Now the needles are magnets.

A needle is made of millions of tiny bits.
Each tiny bit is too small for anyone to see.
These bits are called iron molecules.
Each iron molecule is a tiny magnet.

The tiny magnets are jumbled, helter skelter.
So their magnetism is jumbled too.
And the molecules cannot work together as a magnet.

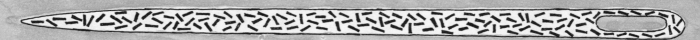

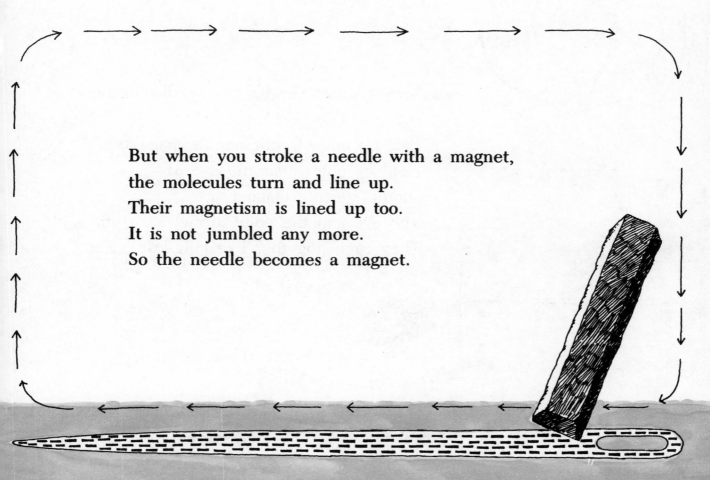

But when you stroke a needle with a magnet,
the molecules turn and line up.
Their magnetism is lined up too.
It is not jumbled any more.
So the needle becomes a magnet.

Now you can see if your needle magnets really work.
Pick up one of your needle magnets.
Hold its point near the eye of another needle magnet.
The eye and the point attract each other.
They come together like long-lost friends.

Now hold its point near the point of
another needle magnet.
The needle rolls away!
Its point is pushed away — repelled — by
the point of the needle magnet in your hand.
That is because they are both magnets.

Try your needle magnet with a plain needle —
one that is not magnetized.
See if the needle magnet repels the plain needle.
It won't, because the plain needle is not a magnet.

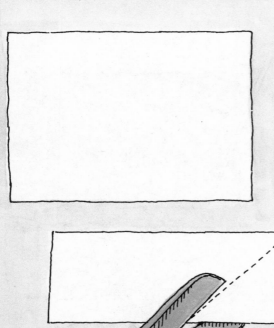

Now cut a piece of paper.
Fold it in half. Cut a point at one end.
Push a magnetized needle into each side.
Be sure both needle points are at the
pointed end of the paper.

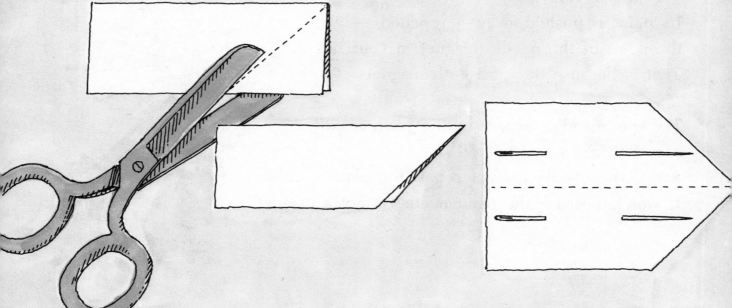

Push the eye of a plain needle
into a piece of clay.

Now lay the paper on top of the plain needle.
Balance it carefully.
You have made your magnet detector.

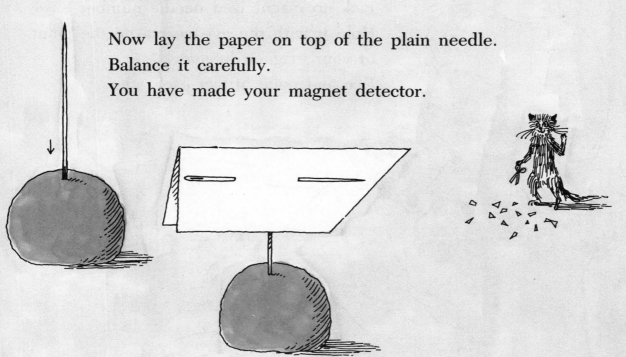

Detecting with Your Detector

Pick up magnetized needle number 3.
Hold it with the eye near a needle point
of your magnet detector.
Eye and point attract each other.

Now try point and point.
The magnet detector moves
away from the needle magnet.
It is repelled.

How about eye and eye?
The same thing happens.
They repel each other.

That's how we can tell a magnet.
One end *attracts* the end
of another magnet.
The other end *repels*.

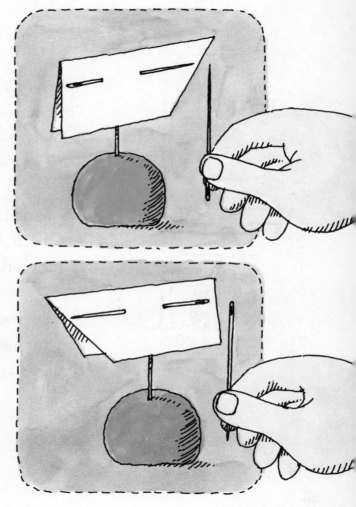

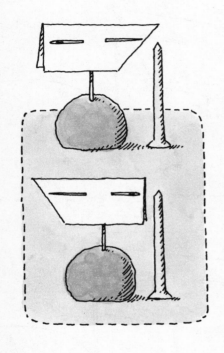

Now you're ready for the great magnet hunt.
Your house is loaded with magnets.
Nobody can find them without a magnet detector.
So start snooping around with yours.

Try a nail, for example.
Are both ends of your detector attracted to it?
If they are, the nail is *not* a magnet.

Maybe you will find a nail that attracts one end
of your magnet detector but repels the other.
If that happens, then the nail is a magnet.

Now try your magnet detector on other things.
If one end is attracted and the other end
is repelled, you have found a magnet.
If both ends are attracted,
you have found plain iron or steel.
But you have not found a magnet.
And if neither end is attracted or repelled,
you have not even found iron or steel.

Time Out for a Boat Race or Two

Only magnets can repel each other.
That's how you know when you have found a magnet.
One end of it attracts your magnet detector.
The other end repels.

That's how a magnet detector works.
And that's how a magnetic boat works too.
You can take time out from your magnet hunt
to have a magnetic boat race.

Cut a boat out of a milk carton.

Push a magnetized needle in to make a mast.

The eye of the needle is below the boat.

Cut a little paper sail for your boat.

Put it in a basin of water — gently.

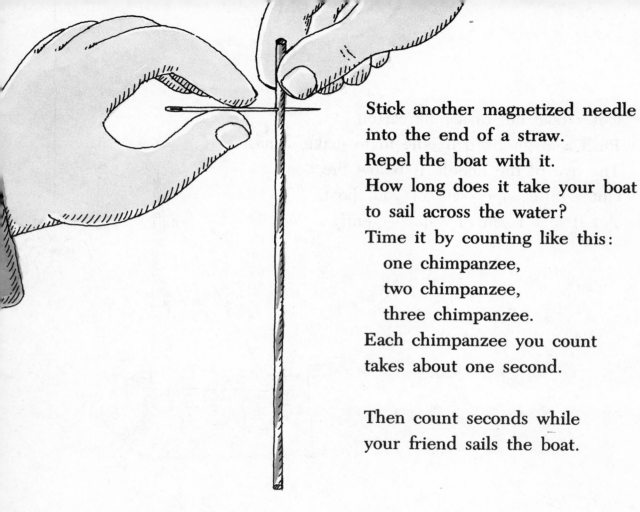

Stick another magnetized needle
into the end of a straw.
Repel the boat with it.
How long does it take your boat
to sail across the water?
Time it by counting like this:
  one chimpanzee,
  two chimpanzee,
  three chimpanzee.
Each chimpanzee you count
takes about one second.

Then count seconds while
your friend sails the boat.

Make some more magnetized needles
and have another kind of boat race.

Drop five pennies in the water.
Start one boat at penny 1
and sail it to 2, 3, 4, and 5.
Start the other boat at 5
and sail it to 4, 3, 2, and 1.
Look out for trouble at penny 3!

Back to the Magnet Hunt

Which room in your house has the most magnets?
A bathroom? A bedroom? The kitchen?
Find out with your magnet detector.

Some iron things are easy to test.
It is easy to test a screw driver.
Check both ends of the iron part.

29

Some iron things are harder to test.
To test a floor lamp, move the detector
slowly, top to bottom.

Watch closely.
Does the magnet detector turn around
when it is part of the way down the lamp?
Then the lamp is a magnet.

But if one end keeps pointing to the lamp,
the lamp is plain iron.

Some iron things are hidden in the walls.
There is an iron box behind a light switch.
Some boxes are magnetized, others are not.
Move your magnet detector slowly, from
top to bottom, from side to side.
If the detector turns around, you have
found a magnetized box.

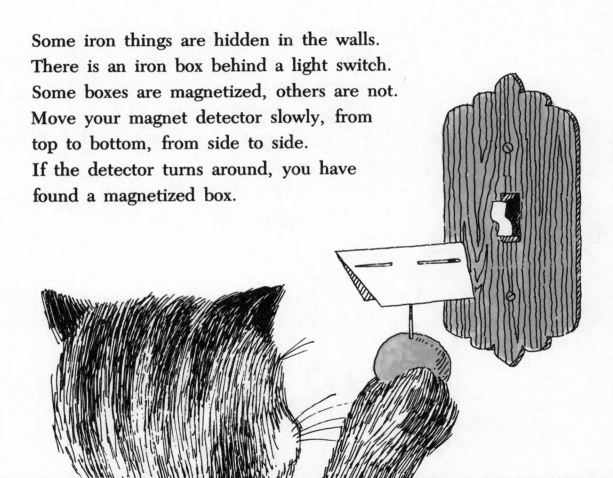

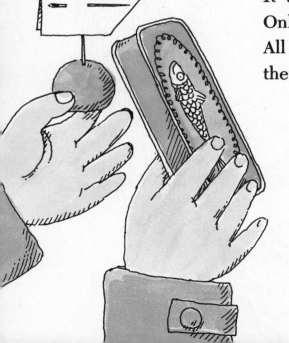

Some things may surprise you.
Would you guess that a sardine can is a magnet?
If it hasn't been moved for a few days,
it is almost surely a magnet!
It will repel one end of your magnet detector.
Only magnets can repel.
All cans become magnetized when
they lie on a shelf for a few days.

A Magnet Mystery

Cans, nails, knives, pins.
There are thousands of things made of iron
and steel in your house.
Many of them are magnets.
They were not specially made to be magnets.
How did they get that way?

Here's a way to find out how
so many things turn into magnets.

Lay a small piece of paper on your bar magnet.
Put a plain needle on the paper.
Leave it there for five minutes.
Test the needle with your detector.
The needle has become a magnet!

You didn't rub the needle with the magnet.
You didn't even touch the needle with the magnet.
The needle was near the magnet and that was enough.
The needle became magnetized.

What about the cans and the knife and the nails
and all the other iron things you tested?
What made some of them become magnets?
Is there a magnet somewhere
that magnetized them?

Magnet Earth

The whole earth is a big magnet!
The earth's magnetism reaches everywhere.
It reaches through the walls and
magnetizes your kitchen knife.
It sweeps into your kitchen cupboard
and magnetizes the tin cans.

It reaches up to mountain tops and
magnetizes steel flagpoles.
With enough time, it will magnetize
anything made of iron or steel.

Magnetism is not the same
in every part of a magnet.
You can see that for yourself.
How many paper clips can you hang
from the ends of your bar magnet?

You can't hang any from the middle.
The paper clips are pulled away
by the magnetism at the ends.
The strongest magnetism comes from the ends.
These ends are called the magnetic poles.

The earth, too, has magnetic poles.
The earth's strongest magnetism is at the poles.

One pole is far north in Canada.
It is called the North Magnetic Pole.

The other pole is far south
in Antarctica.
It is called the South Magnetic Pole.

How do we know the earth is a magnet?
How do we know it has magnetic poles?
Because we have magnet detectors.

Look at the one you made.
When it is not near any other magnet,
it always points the same way.

40

One end points to the North Magnetic Pole.
The other end points to the South Magnetic Pole.
Slowly push the magnet detector
to one side and let it go.
The magnet detector swings back!
It points the same way it did before you pushed it.
The earth's magnetism brings it back.

A Compass Shows the Way

A compass is a magnet detector too.
That's because the needle
in a compass is magnetized.
A compass is easier to carry than
the magnet detector you made.
And it is easier to use.

When you turn a compass around slowly,
the needle stays still.
You can turn it until the N is under
the dark side of the needle.
That way is north.
If you know which way is north, you can
find south, east, and west.

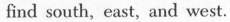

If you have a compass, take it outside.
Use it to find north, east, south, and west.
Which side of your house faces north?
Which side faces east? south? west?

Walk up to the corner of your street
and turn into the next one.
What happens to the compass?

Turn around in a complete circle.
Even if you go all the way around the block,
the compass will always point the same way.
It will point the same way if you walk
in the woods — or if you go out in a boat.
When you use a compass, you can always
find north, east, south, and west.

Magnets, Magnets Everywhere

The world is full of magnets.
There are billions of tiny ones in a compass.
There are billions of tiny ones in your bar magnet.
Your house is full of magnets.
Some were made specially to be magnets.
Some were made into magnets by
the biggest magnet of all —
the whole big earth!

If your compass gets weak,
lay it next to the magnet for an hour,
and it will get strong again.